The Table and The Chair

a poem by Edward Lear   pictures by Tom Powers

HarperCollinsPublishers

The Table and the Chair
Text by Edward Lear
Illustrations copyright © 1993 by Tom Powers
Printed in the U.S.A. All rights reserved.
1 2 3 4 5 6 7 8 9 10
❖
First Edition

Library of Congress Cataloging-in-Publication Data
Lear, Edward, 1812–1888.
    The table and the chair / a poem by Edward Lear ; pictures by Tom
Powers.
        p.   cm.
    Summary: A table and a chair decide to take a walk but soon lose their
way and are escorted home by a duck, a mouse, and a beetle.
    ISBN 0-06-020804-X. — ISBN 0-06-020805-8 (lib. bdg.)
    1. Children's poetry, English.   [1. English poetry.   2. Nonsense verses.
3. Furniture—Poetry.]   I. Powers, Tom (Tom J.), ill.
II. Title.
PR4879.L2T33   1993   91-45538
821' .8—dc20   CIP
                                                    AC

For Amy and Emma

Said the Table to the Chair,
"You can hardly be aware,
How I suffer from the heat,
And from chilblains on my feet!
If we took a little walk,
We might have a little talk!
Pray let us take some air!"
Said the Table to the Chair.

Said the Chair unto the Table,

"Now you know we are not able!

How foolishly you talk,

When you know we cannot walk!"

Said the Table, with a sigh,

"It can do no harm to try,

I've as many legs as you,

Why can't we walk on two?"

So they both went slowly down,
And walked about the town

With a cheerful bumpy sound,

As they toddled round and round.

And everybody cried,
As they hastened to their side,

"See! The Table and the Chair
Have come out to take the air!"

But in going down an alley,

To a castle in a valley,

They completely lost their way,

And wandered all the day,

Till, to see them safely back,
They paid a Ducky-quack,

Who took them to their house.

Then they whispered to each other,

"O delightful little brother!

What a lovely walk we've taken!

Let us dine on Beans and Bacon!"

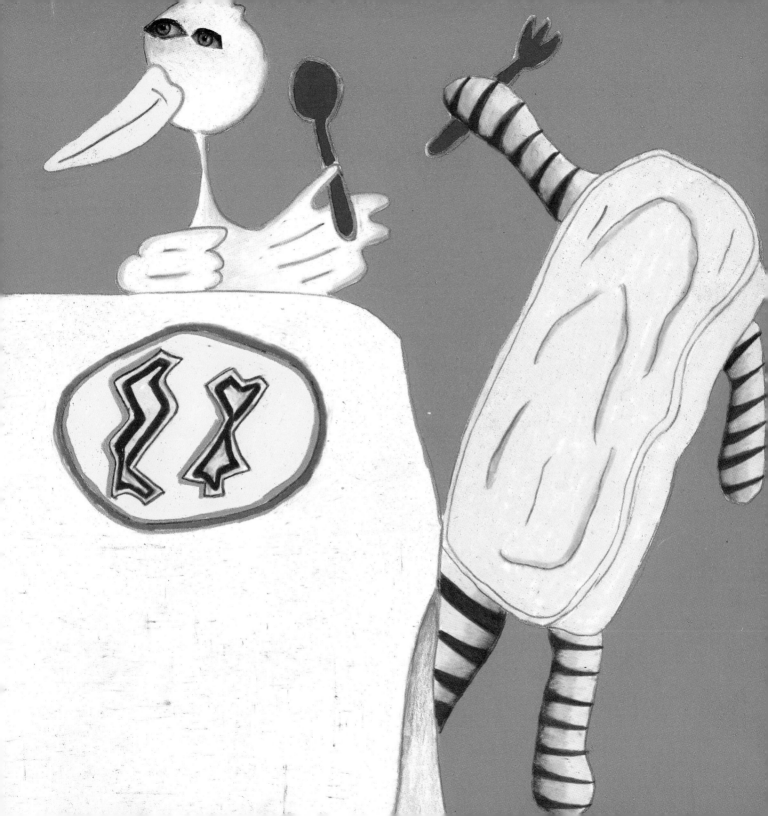

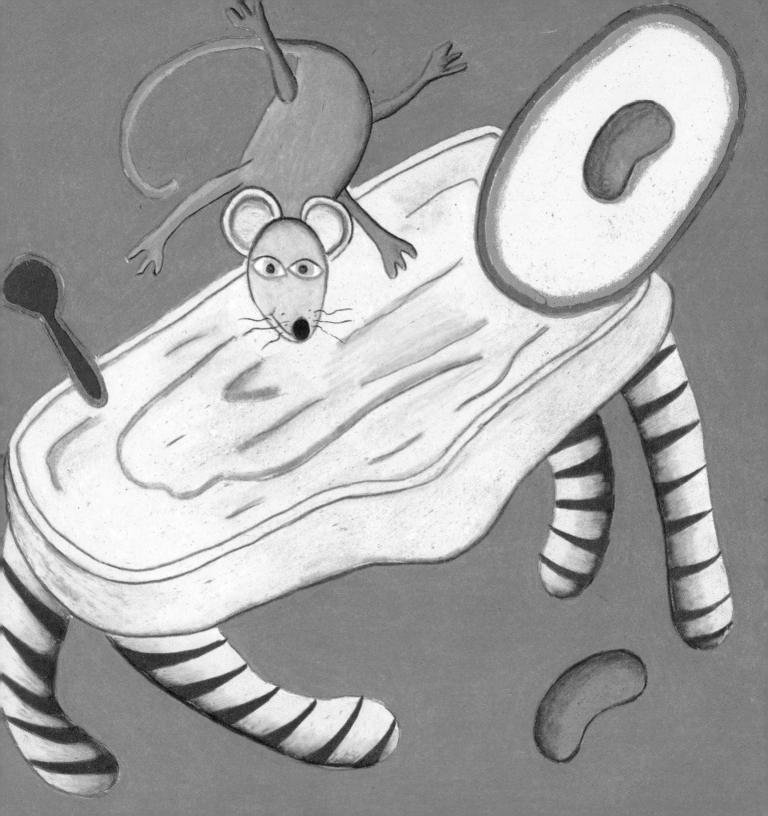

So the Ducky, and the leetle

Browny-Mousy and the Beetle

Dined, and danced upon their heads

Till they toddled

to their beds

THE TABLE and THE CHAIR

Said the Table to the Chair,
"You can hardly be aware,
How I suffer from the heat,
And from chilblains on my feet!
If we took a little walk,
We might have a little talk!
Pray let us take some air!"
Said the Table to the Chair.

Said the Chair unto the Table,
"Now you know we are not able!
How foolishly you talk,
When you know we cannot walk!"
Said the Table, with a sigh,
"It can do no harm to try,
I've as many legs as you,
Why can't we walk on two?"

So they both went slowly down,
And walked about the town
With a cheerful bumpy sound,
As they toddled round and round.
And everybody cried,
As they hastened to their side,
"See! The Table and the Chair
Have come out to take the air!"

But in going down an alley,
To a castle in a valley,
They completely lost their way,
And wandered all the day,
Till, to see them safely back,
They paid a Ducky-quack,
And a Beetle, and a Mouse,
Who took them to their house.

Then they whispered to each other,
"O delightful little brother!
What a lovely walk we've taken!
Let us dine on Beans and Bacon!"
So the Ducky, and the leetle
Browny-Mousy and the Beetle
Dined, and danced upon their heads
Till they toddled to their beds.

About the Poet

Edward Lear (1812–1888) was born in London.
He lived for many years in Italy and frequently
traveled, visiting Corsica, Corfu, Sicily,
Turkey, and India to gather material
to write travel books. His first
collection of verse, published
in 1846, was called BOOK OF
NONSENSE, and he went on to
write and illustrate several
other volumes of nonsense
songs and poems for
children and adults
to enjoy.

About the Artist

Tom Powers grew up in Peru
and Mexico before coming to the
United States, where he received his B.F.A.
degree from Maryland Institute College of Art and
his M.F.A. degree from Queens College, N.Y. His art has been
exhibited in many galleries and museums. He has played in a rock and
roll band, and he used to make a living drawing pictures of shoes for a weekly
newspaper. Mr. Powers is a carpenter, and he teaches art history and color theory.

99133

Ja
Lear
The table and the chair

5/94   16.00